The Damage

NEW AND SELECTED POEMS

DREW MILNE was born in Edinburgh, Scotland 1964. His previous books of poetry include *Sheet Mettle* (1994), *How Peace Came* (1994), *Songbook* (1996), *Bench Marks* (1998), *As It Were* (1998), *familiars* (1999), *Pianola* (2000) and *The Gates of Gaza* (2000). Having previously been a lecturer at the universities of Edinburgh and Sussex, he is currently the Judith E. Wilson Lecturer in Drama and Poetry, Faculty of English, University of Cambridge. He edits the imprint *Parataxis Editions* and the journal *Parataxis: modernism and modern writing*.

Also by Drew Milne

Satyrs and Mephitic Angels (Cambridge: Equipage, 1993)
Sheet Mettle (London: Alfred David Editions, 1994)
How Peace Came (Cambridge: Equipage, 1994)
Carte Blanche (Kenilworth: Prest Roots Press, 1996)
Songbook (Kirkcaldy: Akros, 1996)
Bench Marks (London: Alfred David Editions, 1998)
As It Were (Cambridge: Equipage, 1998)
familiars (Cambridge: Equipage, 1999)
Pianola, with Jo Milne (Cambridge: REM Press, 2000)
The Gates of Gaza (Cambridge: Equipage, 2001)
Mars Disarmed (Barrington, M.A.: The Figures, 2002)

The Damage

NEW AND SELECTED POEMS

DREW MILNE

SALT

PUBLISHED BY SALT PUBLISHING
PO Box 202, Applecross, Western Australia 6153
PO Box 937, Great Wilbraham, Cambridge PDO CB1 5JX United Kingdom

First published 2001

Printed and bound in the United Kingdom by Lightning Source

Typeset in Swift 9.5 / 13

British Library Cataloguing-in-Publication Data
A catalogue record for this book is available from the British Library
ISBN 1 876857 11 0 paperback

SP

1 3 5 7 9 8 6 4 2

For Rachel

Contents

Acknowledgements

The Damage includes poems from a range of books, chapbooks and previously unpublished poems. They are arranged more or less in chronological order of composition. My thanks in particular go to Rod Mengham, the publisher of the Equipage pamphlets *Satyrs and Mephitic Angels*, *How Peace Came*, *As It Were* and *familiars*, and to Ian Hunt, the publisher of *Sheet Mettle* and *Bench Marks*. I am also grateful to Duncan Glen, who first published *Songbook* in chapbook form. *How Peace Came* is presented here in a different version from that previously published as part of an installation devised in conjunction with Andrew James. *Lullay*, *Quite Contrary*, *Gloss* and *Accidents* were written in collaboration with artwork by Jo Milne. Gratitude unbound goes to Chris Emery for all his patience and labour in the making of this book.

Versions of these poems first saw the dark and light in the following journals and anthologies: *Zed 2 0*, *Parataxis*, *C.C.C.P. 3 Programme*, *Angel Exhaust*, *Purge*, *Comparative Criticism*, *Edinburgh Review*, *Southfields*, *Poetry Review*, *Salt*, *Kunapipi*, *The Gig*, *Angle*, *inscape*, *Jacket* & *100 Days*. My thanks to Simon Jarvis, Andrew Duncan, Robert Hampson, David Kinloch, Gavin Wallace, Richard Price, Peter Forbes, John Kinsella, Brian Lucas, Leonard Brink, Nate Dorward, John Tranter, and Andrea Brady.

Dolphin Song

Would I were as Arion, or as the story told,
choosing harp fish swordpens to take the plank, the egg,
the swallowing passion in supperless *díke*.

Where is that dolphin now? we still adhere to the
doctrine of redemption which originally
connoted a slave purchasing his liberty:

not to change its world but to escape this, it has
flown off the wheel, off grief's thole misery while vine
sprays against are its expenses. For dolphin song

no season supposes such slavery orphic,
while urban revolution remains roused as lyres
for the hungry he hath filled with such good things, of

which one among is hunger *anánke*, potlach
expenses defrayed deformist, details lacking
as if normal proceeding will follow slaughter,

or our harmony parts dissolve clear and brittle.

Daymares

It was easier to keep on than wait for days
to shorter get, allowing night speak day-mares their
turn to rust amicably amid thoughts silting hope;

no imagined that could not falter, needing nights
back to imagine with when the city silts too,
searching for what unseemly newness, unsilted still,

to save a heat where satire crumbles, or a past
catching on to this new temerity, its weight
of action as rusts no longer amicable.

There is no bleak suffice, no text unbound to bleakness,
as would be, when all around lose theirs. *Come clearer!*
no suffice could unyet or relinquish injury,

want, so many little deaths, boring the shiners
upon quick graves of angers, or is it lonely
passing among without heed for exile therein.

Don't suppose, would it, that by-the-by clocks off, while
awash in daymares and nighting lamps of waste our
goods selling bads the very dregs knew odious:

discussion is waged on alarmist, in alerts,
by sofa or by crook, or *sang froid* pachyderms,
but raptured hurtwise tracks regret *to hope dusting!*

as in truth to say mourn for the past circumvents.

Through the buy-out jargon

I am virus soul corp, hug me to this unreal
viral city which had not thought, death undone, so
short term many fun-funding were this captive class;

for our soul libidinal pulsations referred,
hush fund breezes cyclone my well-products esquire,
or are greenfield ventures as this stock cubism falls.

I am aid pack, cash-crop and pearl mint tax heaven
with airs, seedcorns, graces skeltering pro or fits,
yours contumely, or old use-value as am used;

but cashing chips one in, figaro appliqué,
these now machine tools bitter this dream crop decor,
appellation cash vortex, wonders contrôlée,

as atrium hollows words which do not pass go.

Positive Indiscriminations

The male my hermit and manner view, or it ill
be easier to amble you, as sod the count's
odd sadeian bosom: that twizzle of velour

authenticity ligs on diners card before
currying distemper: *thus fresco!* as it grew
too astart its vile pink and mildew narcissus.

Your after personal lather shaves conditions to
the grain, and sandal would glows penumbra, like raised
faculties lathed to *is it me you're looking for?*

I'll be buggered doubt if it ill be easier
to trekky from cling-on to boldly woe, wrecky
from hornblower, as my toy captain flies undone

to the oh so moby dick. Stand out in flux, my
chassis, *go getty get two!* where a rival peers
so in dissidence are personality glues.

Can it for cried out loud be ill, this bolster blust,
where muzzles so militant are discriminate
particular wars losing dots to incisions?

Woe aquamarine boy ogles a-gloop, fish tank
a-breathing, *might as well* plunder your theme tune's youth,
breeding goggles as Irish masques unflint the stones

which are teething *the Troubles* in this Trumpet town,
as glorious good would await the orange monsoon
marching season: *will it be veiled rivers of blood,*

or the world well lost, washing soldiers dreams to the
foot of iambs? How now, brown cow, sacred brownie
of a cubbish clout, will it come in bull-dog chants?

My wall to wall crumbles, fondling what its falling
reason suffices, and I'll Hemingway in slow
motion, if you'll be mine buster, this double oh

sever me shaken and lotus-bond stirred: it's me,
yes flirty, *oi polloi*, and I'll fame you baby,
like no transcendental *epoche* ever could.

Camera my maybe as I fleet it to crashing
guitars! and sheer out to one big man walk for one
kind man, in head-brides revisited while gloaming

cities groom unquiet, but as mental suers
gutter-press it, I am as ill as resources:
does it feel good renouncing discrimination?

I bet! *Well I'll be*, belower me willingly,
I canute not these kingly waves, but despair the
eponymous women and children from sieges,

while old uncurl dunder-bluss is the unveiled pause
of all kiss, whose lips chrome the enemy salvoes
training in play boy plasticine pavlov artwork.

Still it looks like trouble, *it looks like there'll be more*,
but candle my armour random bores, I'm just an
amicable man, who spays distance aargh moor dusts

of uppishness and beaches lust spermaceti
for *hope the mastodon*, spolia opima
of reason's amble to homo erectus, as

veiled shaft members ingrate diction shamble it so.
Passed out to out pretty, *I know you* the *son*, my
fathead farmer will be as worn by the hand-downs,

aging deceased repent! But as no demiurge
I'll libertine time in gnostic bliss, or is it
blisters, it harm you will harmly done, yes blisters,

calmant to the sleepless still caffeine trot, and thus
zealot erectus, homing my consensus, if
not saving face secrets himself is man, or would

as awe man for awe that *me you're looking for* is.

In Memoriam Joseph Beuys

1.

In gripe lore rumbles war among moderns
     the humble it dreams wet
these hold all penchants for how to pay
     lisp your r around Rimbaud and go all
impresario mon juste
       for thieving abates
but not the look as contemporary mingles it
howl mid-atlantic coyote
     fat sucker lush
likes Beuys like Beuys likes publicity so
    this even if Andy troubles
what with what politics *what's yours?*
as fifth international slow gloats demise
consolidates inc
      among diverse others
slow boating it to audience participation
    behind you! in chat show chews
we're warming up for pause core grain-
less sepia relents in cut up
    burrows *all together now!*
sweating last human pieces my contact
         there faded
sepia genitals in tattoo smile from old calendar
    relents still to *in the know*
shining in my irony plated social kills
nice to see you yes it's delicious
wishing seconds like no felt tomorrow
    slow down the pratfalls
harmony guise shines freeze innuendo and
hurrah for applause man standards we can
    on cue *like it!* Dalai Lama cosmetic
as answer drifted back over remote mine-
lands of a dead star not very
call me cute
call me what the hell you laugh for canned.

2.

It's all hands on ship my feckless sea persons
drop curtains we'll futurist in rich disturbance
ahoy art-less! viral shows shout against those
we're Just-In-Time that's JIT! for go-slow
        All out! our future ist franchised
        down sound bites ye petty *bouge pas!*
    pun along a few don'ts on Sunday we bleed
or shallow it through to mid price laments
        toads of woad hole you bore us
we'll go all eco art trash cosy if you don't
    sit up and pay cable
    subscribe there *follow the leader!*
we'll be no ad man's throb flush prize job
twitching to first over the wall corp ego
        our sounds bite back fat sucker
    jealous Maecenas from slash cut prices
the Texas in memoriam trophy shudders
to the standard oils of Folger juniors
get out of conglomerates get into Shakespeare
        ye olde facsimile hoards *it pays!*
        a word from our sponsoring angels
award your bliss markets and *get compact!*
or is that weariness rather than perspectival
spread-sheet autocue *ho, ho! on camera one*
    you mean we never meant
    it that play so fast we must
    scratch ahead the wireless
accustomed to the sped words *buy now!*
no dirge but in mono-breath jive talk junk
    you groove we track
    encomiums and viral breath
    blows its own sales to sirens
this is your life the bellows wheeze where none
    coyote howls to straw ideology without ideas
cloudy in places where these scattered showers
purpling in damask sash that nought a muses.

3.

Jelly roll fat pack culture strolls complete
on I don't know but yep it's all here in grey
for a live one saddest of all moving pictures
  just listen and underwear charming
pants off I'll flag mine to *see the tie slip!*
dialogue yep surety sure
     wait your snatch through meals
for more hot dinners than we have feed back
    it's in the pink
  but even comes a turn to eat mics
you'll speak like journal pit bull scholion
avante! avante! the changing of the guard
  me fat sucker – you coyote *dig it!*
all substrates to the impresario gel
    neo-neon *check that, alright!*
teeth to the chisel eyes right
    storm troop to pithy apocalypse
quick march as masochism ghosts mountain
    wherever whenever we gather
there's always one cries *yeah!* among us
  cut up amid prelates howl on those
unspeakably long lines no agenbite sounds
   done the work *get it?* know stuff
as corpses oeuvre it to blessed philologist
in double-breasted Achilles-mouth harm-
ony for its next trick *please, you're too kind*
  while indianola instrumental novelty
  fox trots to *Every Kiss is the Same*
    how's that coyote?
speak up cry wolf no metaphor murder but
roll on worldly lit. bugs jiggering *no really!*
gathered here amid self-publicity
   hymn me
  our text is *Tonite!*
  your host is shame
and the art of psalmody de profundis I belch.

Lullay

Water churns,
radiating the distance;
alive in a vicarious future
into uncouth world icommen ertou,
which gets on
          with humming along backgrounds
to atmosphere hiss of sulphureous skies,
as rubber
          rumbling of carburettors
abbreviates
          the night illumination.
There is no easy stumble to dismay,
lollay, lollay, to car ertou bemette;
all must falter,
       glad-handed into praise,
          into the ruins of realism
where, amid a stray
        rust screech of axle,
we seems an orchard refrain,
             combusting
with don'ts,
       and, hatched back to carbon static,
don't is all the charge attrition distilled.

Quite Contrary

Swete lemmon,
        wormes woweth under cloud
as hallowed spoons
        cuddle
                        these silver racks,
so soft cherry fair
                is out of kilter;
but brush low,
        the tackle is
                sweeping still,
where the call
                goes to die before sleeping;
but each gome glit forth as a guest only
in angry mists
                of loaming
                care-weeds
cherish the dull
        as how our garden grows
new skin eruptions,
    groans,
                        will wart wrinkles,
ears all cauliflower to Castaly,
while swete
                lashes of I,
        resting,
                        as if
there is more rancour in the dust flying.

Gloss

Cats-eyes clouding over
           turning   gloss tears
to shine
        each shifting
             autumnless halo,
mushrooming into the creeping overgrowth
of endless braid,
        as the gilted lapels
hold me
      from the halo headed wardens,
who read the matted floor as woven
                  grids,
where small scale
        mosaic
        enclosures
persist in such corrosive atmospheres
that the choking tears
          knows its street bib
is all software,
      shuffling to
      weeping lines,
as the saying goes,
    and texture   refrains.

Accidents

The snail of slaughter passes
                   through the dream
or order,
        showering its lost tickets
all the way round
        the skirting cattle traps,
as gig lamps breathe prowlers,
                   the bullet trains,
the harvest of iron,
        rolled out to chip-sewn
thinness,
        for dancing bird-men with speech-scrolls
and lost relatives:
                   or at any rate,
blood-letting deemed acceptable
                        in stone
caught as petroleum film on lip-stained
cups,
        where we find evidence of the love
of polychromatic effects
                   contrived
by inlaying
        and, conversely, crash scratches
in reliefs, so called,
            unnaturally   exposed.

A still life in blue

Key in your chosen sore digit light codes,
as asphalt on blue notes, or pin connects
there to ease, is lay numbers, an affray
turning savoury or blanched / as I would
                have it, and am vulgar
                with pensionable posts,
                ground and down a grand
piano we call the last waltz through the
institutions. Still you catch a mid-frieze,
a rift, whim or sundry windlass in awkward
name squads tuned in drops of out, the out-looks
                bleached, come all overcome,
                resting sherry on yawns,
                as per fucking usual,
while famine stalks rash dispensing kindness.
One stone into the beach clears flock circles
where sandboys blether geodesic laughs,
the last on these no-hoping scorn dancers
turning where the rash begins. Where do the
yellow lines start to quiver, break surface
aghast or harshly tendered out, lose brave
and face all arteries, all passion fruit
and all the lust accrued without design.
                If is hardly the party
                to which were invited   ⸰
                all the old hopes / none.
                Lungs cry slurry, asbestos,
                then mesothelioma
brushes the known roof of this construction
with premature dust related ill-ease,
then unremembered dies. I don't hear it
any more than the sky respects yellow
lines drawn across its long loss of music,
where airs dance into the unconsoled rooms
without which thoughts of those already dead
have no cadence or respite from wishes.

If you would, it could be
perhaps this last perhaps,
sarcasm kissed
as sarcasm does,
its minor artforms
blowing death blushes,
which visible thorns remind us is dark,
as all the seriousness I yearn for tries
to let bliss in on the secret. Once more
the red rust of the night sky seems human,
or humanly lit by spark and light trains
trundling awareness and so much harsh freight
that clotted scars, eyeless, dark flowing blood
may curdle the calm to scorn, as I do.
A chain letter courts your close affluence
in human affairs, asking the diagram
which laughs back, what it is to be hoped for
and can be done, what it is to be loved
where a group breathing calm stills the light fit
embrace of a memory song, a first
flush choir in this possible power.
                  Don't will be this slogan,
                  curling around the grievous
                  bodily harmonies, where
                  music is as music does,
where the mean time foresees a lengthy close,
and where red army choristers release
their agent purple loves. As around gills
of salmon drinking tanker blood, a dash
to mediocrity sucks new smoothness
while abhorrence wells in wet gravity:
                  this *now* suppurates,
                  this negative equity
                  of fouling penitence,
                  falling grouts with the lies
of fast statues a particular scorn,
for what now will kill these ease chariots
of star-struck news casting seamers, remorse
in absent-minded city, where once but

pity, is blush decadence now gone grime.
                    Arise sweet fire of tempers,
                    thorns in upper hall
                    picture moss, blaze resin
                    in scars of tithes dripping still
with meagre truth stipends played hereabouts;
throw frieze knots to cloistered embroidery
of such poached hope, ivory blessed charm-schools.
Chattering class, pine on arrogant pie;
blend on, quaff fluted slave sung righteousness,
                    while happier walls
                    might fly through breeze,
                    these cobbles crush, and trees
                    hum bomb ballast drones.
The sun baked velvet of revolution
might coordinate our tepid dissents
in catatonia, as graphs are bliss:
there maps the lost symphonies, tone dismay,
comes on fresh but is all over, happy
as we who sold this free, this crocus called
defame, sold lays to flee obliquity
or mumbling sing of shame. But crash / this quill
conforms to bills in awe commanding flaws,
leech-love until no purpose stills the glow-
worms tricked in gauze who will have brutal force;
                    trees hum sweet subsidence
                    rivers chanted for oil wars,
                    or shoots at the holy fruit
                    of blood stone planted.
Loose leaf meets blade and gravely weighs flagrant
winter tourists, whose psalms on trade now roast
and fade a rash on dry forests. Still none
                    be so in harmless no
                    that dreams a curse refined,
                    whose glaze grows patina
                    or dusting slow, varnishes
the blind weasel bluff of street-wise word husks,
a size it little profits to bust. Still/
famine eyes in grainless sighs fall brittle

or nonplussed, while every state meant murmur
creates the wash and blends in airless hate.
This world awaits a glaze of angel pens,
but I renounce weapons of happiness
and the petals of blood which kiss such hope-
less greener grassless: 'Shoot into the foot,
I say, and only then into the air.'

A modest preposition
for the people of East Timor

Gnosis means simply knowledge, of whither
we are hastening, though in other times
it is as if one met song murderers,
death hands whose sacrifice is body fact.
              It is not so difficult
              to see the advance stand still
              on circle line excursions,
swan-dancing over the pre-scribed pages
still cultivated as our last chapter,
whose neck turn thought is to be all the same
              though its pain never is,
              while the tread 'essential'
              is nought but read ends,
where that something to be said is here blown
before an altar of bad-mouthing calm
that has every thus crust appearance
of being consecrated now to prose;
              perhaps a sophist delight
              first composed dissoi logoi,
              if fraught, mark the old turn,
with the vengeance of communication
whose firsts are a thousand island dressing
cooked in fine archaic illustration.
The result is a disaster, flesh lows
              as the spits turn critical,
              the state of delirium
              signs its fault, and its purpose,
like so much else politic dullness, is
not to cure one single flesh rash richness,
much less deliver us from the old stall
              of some moment dress
              whose tardy expatiation
              is a fashion of *other*.
In a very framework of city, law,
or our covering stillness, is only

a drift, striving to obscure that poor will
the polis spent its meaning creating,
>   like whether to wage slaughter
>   or just send observers:
>   our own plenty questions
>   face us like blocked capital,
apologies on part half of people
do not ring true, and besides, nothing here
indicates what is still called election,
as to pass, from divided opinion
to bloody confrontation, is rather
>   the current of this *stasis*.
>   In the other form of trance,
>   on sponsored Dionysus
or the bold insomnia of sold news,
the wine has a happy dish, with brilliant
shivers drunk deep, singing home sweet heimat.
>   A clumsy proposal, then,
>   for the swift abolition
>   of *all* our advertising
>   from cable to leader and hope,
>   whose possible first pleasure
>   may be a beginning
>   on vultureless beauty
drained of litanies and winged messengers
whose further angels assist the carved drapes
of actually existing capitalism.

A Garden of Tears

'Certain gardens are described as retreats when they are really attacks.'
Ian Hamilton Finlay

i.

It's a long way from love to the state we're in
here where fish are just at sea, and to know is
a law of the land, or any old wonder
as nature calls – *chuchotement* – what the dickens
can such in hope springs diurnal add up to,
or float to, so languid through these crossed channels
where spirit is without duty and knows love
for the state bliss might be when words do wither:
go then, the way of steam ships and dictators,
go then softly, quick to the ends of this life,
ineffably melding where these be pardons
and there such sacrifice is all our hatred,
stored in sand for when stones can be heard to cry
that we fear no more the heat of the trident.

ii.

Out that long dolour look you gave me to wean
this eldritch sadness stills the warm felt of breath
across whose cheek, and in tears, the curfew dries
as hope is salted round the lips in Gaza
stripped only so slowly to earth's hearing bone
that the face fires harsh amber from stone glances
which, once lit, extinguish this float glass plainsong,
or is it just pain in mosaic and jaw:
no, not that wish about the jowl, it is pain,
even the wall is weeping, seeping such rage
that breathing baffles, hung as a cluster of
camphire in the lost vineyards of Engedi,
where unmeasured song is suspended in brine
and barges drift, slightly stale, to the dead sea.

iii.

Better you to me than I were to myself
but what water we were I'm against it still,
the turn on love is patience and thousand lies
while sleepless still loves we cannot sleep still with
are breathless but still lives we cannot breathe with,
til doubt gives in fear and throws the first light stone
against names we never made, and loving break,
our breast plate of sighs in armour of accord:
call it operation bouffe, a taking leave
in lost of means, burnt islands and grimaces,
that's one end or two, a rash passion of notes
whose calm call shall remain nameless, but is law,
where wills are alive with the sound of water,
water of our eyes falling, felt and all told.

iv.

The more is the pity, as to two touching,
any rainbow appears a bridge over war,
even if we do not live, nor even near,
but shuffle such as the colours of money
in the gross nets wading though this vale of tears
where an increase in size of relative debts
makes it *practically* unimaginable
that we can rely on natural forces
to stabilise our interest rates, back on track
where Zeus fuels the milky way of defence costs:
there is one other option, to allow growth
to grow and increase the critical value
of the deficit as a fraction of this
to what is, or what is still and always more.

v.

Well like as maybe, the quite gentle gripe
is like as new lost, place lost in window days
where never knowingly is ever the less,
still under sold over that tread of pages
whose count me in is the harvest epaulette
and sheaves of ornamental treason; our feed
of dutiful mésalliance thinks ring on rung
as our past tense in special offers does fade,
or passes the tell by date with new freedom
to rot spontaneously: you know the rot
I mean, I take it, and savour the flavour
of its passing, into the spirit of mould
where you would love, but let the reason be love,
and just as sure as the turning of the earth.

vi.

Come in the valley of the shadow of breath
where we are this kiss in impossible grief,
that never savoured wrench as now and never
when happen is, the thinking over descant
to once upon each other, folded in sums,
parts in inconstant disarray of ice
as this scream is, an only shade of dismay
that pulls each faceless tooth along to wisdom:
these are our lines upon each blowing birth bruise
dashed to lungs, as skin curls in such heavy fruit,
its lisp already for that day when one dies,
simply leaves, or forgets the flares of always,
left flickering stunned in early fear of now
when each feared for kiss is still a greater death.

vii.

What not curls unknown against the lip split,
spilt quite apart from what cannot wash, and does,
as perils timid flung in held afflatus
where reason grows its only slow friend in pain
and clasps of breath fail, fall then run asunder,
spun through in what parts to remain familiar
or is the part where lightning is nothing new,
is wrung to a crush of what will not wonder:
no, and no wonder you prefer the thunder
where the piano of dull skies falls through stairs
showering air over the broken meadows
which numberless sums of all our breaking parts
even the parting past does not wish for
or cannot hold still in a pity of ears.

viii.

Count in tears through wine how it unwinding downs
out so much as a by your leaving now gone
while pleasures stretch out, bitten into the lost
something, as less of that empty slidden we
who were never this, never this in ease or
in that some kind of forgiveness for the rest,
as would remnants gather to back one's own sill
lying still among dreams there is no wish for
on such melisma drifting scars where there is,
after all, nothing natural about it:
no, not along that light flesh of which we dream
where tight skies are shocking to the blood of tears,
he among hers, she among his and never
but the saw in it, just this each in each saw.

ix.

It's a long way still where love our gulf is war,
here where arks are royal, ripe and for sinking,
our bonds are broke, such tearing kisses, and soil
makes shifts of our futures, a water of dust
whose ashen felt rubble bursts banks on the Clyde,
where we sat down, smiled, and remembered Sion,
or was it cyanide fixed in Prussian blue
of a mind broke in fear that death becomes me,
becomes we who were what falls out together,
as perishing tears tear up the sodding earth:
for as long as the sun takes to set its gloss
the labours of our loss are still glistening,
and where the going is over, gone over,
there we go, slightly pale, to the ends of love.

How Peace Came
for Andrew James

    if I may be so bold
      or night evince
go suck on tip of sour tongue and come in
        into the red
    on purple drum and drag
chained to blown organs of good old Corti
      or casus belli on Balkan toast
    saying blast! deafness!

    the chair is still triste hélas
      and a plague on all your roses
      your soft pate
        and dome

        come into the red
here where crabs are so dishy
  amid rouge stripes slow firing
        amber mouton rage
    lip lash expresso
    pressed citrons crying Papa!
ou fuck that for a laugh Clio
as the cute muse wears mud and cucumber glasses
      bidet on brioche
e-mail mousse setting rust on angel delight

      for Paul Klee

the problem of sonic boom is now clearly
upon us
and in spades
but if I may be so cold
let's rip chords
from a priori harp rooms
and staunch the ripe flow of steady eddies
these king-size ears in eau de calumny
born to backsheesh
for the bloody boom forms a high carpet
and dry cotton
affords no protection

no, and no red ripple to come into
which is about as much as we can take
bars in our eyes
stars in our hearts
and holes on fur
as the chevalier d'industrie
green king on ice
says go and catch a falling plate

and in whipped dreams I'm afraid
for kindred spirits
or who would play savage rumpus
on tap

it's a gas at any rate
in one take and in the can
dido and dada for the under fives
braggadocio in sublime dough
listless myopics to can the noise
a keep down low and rank

piquant flowers on plasticine park
sucking punter's lisp
in art thou heavy breathing
or just good friends
or better still?

no matter no mufti
we're on the wing for sure
if you'll join us
and no place like the better part at bay
so bank on it buddy
till greater pressures force the tube wide open
gales in tiny tots
where dank white trash is hurt neon
like laughter
and we take the air
or more simply fail to swallow
the gall

if I may be so sounded
        come off it
        capital is not late
        nor mature
    nor a higher plant than the weed
        it just grows on you
leaves of paper notes fluttering
        in the annex
        and bonds booming
        in ah, ah domine deus
        we're here for the duration
                suits in clubs
and thanks for having us
                the food was rude

        so how about it
        a peace of action
        feet in drag down the path
    amid red quakes of crazed paving

                mandibles just ajar
                chin up in Mary's garden

                and yer must be kidding
                it will never do
                what with the insurance
                and all hell to pay
            not counting corpses under the grill
                mine's a burger
                with en suite sauce

back on the warm sonant front
    war weariness is all the rage
  a truce for sore ears

  what serene candy

  melts a stern areopagus to butter
    gold capped teeth
who need mastic like a hold in the head

      their standing armies
    gone right to the mirth's surface
      lank curlews struck dumb
    a sluice passing ports
      gin slings
        then fizzy bombs

    kindly wipe your feet on my soul
      before you come in
      into the red
    from coccyx to cochlea
      where glow notes go
and more privy in the bush than on a vice hand
      shaken to its ends
    dust bowls rung on bugger all gongs
      pity as pap says
    the world's not a fair race
      so give over
        if I may be so old

all aboard!
once bitten twice blithe
rouble-breasted spirit!
you have so many ways of drinking us
to the lees
but is that Europe in your package
or are you just pleased to fleece us Jason?

deep fangs sunk in legoverland
going like a dump trunk
a melt down
mars in vice
for we are the way we go to it

get artic'late baby
there's a super highway passing through you
don't be a nimby
not in my black yarn
cuss cup and garrotted
in worsted threads of axle grease
and thimble

hey asda!
you're a plonker
grunging the motorcade
or blocking soft lows and beta
that's Alph
liminal wet stuff
and hooded grace

will someone tell that tambourine man
    to turn it down?

        it's more than flesch can bare its brass to

            a ray fawning
            in brash diamante glory
        we can't hear ourselves blink
            for open neck sweaters and bream
        the heart rackets and rattle cries
            of Eat Gucci!
            bowl and cowl and gore
            now the hail is hard as
            meat balls

            ah bisto
            what's cooking Titus?
        sock it to me like you do
            on tusk and tiramisu
    oh move over soft now lady
        or they'll love you to death

            which reminds me
        fancy taking a king's soggy biscuit?

cool tank tops with Scottish widows
        man, the gear's terrific
            such a blooming dark habit
                becomes you

as sky falls into global muff
wrapped around in melanin tans
in fax of fuzz box
there's mud in your lie

are you feared of creatures
such as that slunk yawn
of art thou slow dancing

unprepared to leave space for air
beneath the flow of bodies
whisked to viper
for the hair you breathe
clasping your untipped
furry tongue

no way no snake bite
just forked tongue
on doggy brek
get that down you
pic 'n' mix herbaceous borders
freshed off Balkan smorgasbord
oh but it does you good to go suck tartan
weight off your pins
as the clutch goes off the risus purus
chocs and spleen away
countdown and left off!
to the end of our
common era

dinosaurs are us
stuff the red commie peppers
go into black vests
it's all the rage
a quote sir?
'you can't run a revolution in a suit and tie'
yeah I hear what you're braying
pornocrat sud
go blonde lagoon
hoppit Scotch git
marg wouldn't melt on your silver tonsils
or moss pap
just suck it and see

the mint with the cold war in the middle
is where the bucks stop
def minky and jaws
fin-soup or arch culls
though the ecu in your hand is worth
all the rosey gun teeth and dripping

such hard lard
felt old
consistency of flesch
soft to burn

but dad, what's the moon meant to
advertise? and can I have some
for afters

no way no beagle bender
    up the wall and over the counter
we'll see seams of rags
    in stitches
        barely visible
from our seat here among falling clouds
    in gambolling amber dawns

        it's a barking ballet
        it's a ballroom blitz

          pssst!
        wanna buy a bazooka?
fresh out of spinach pyjamas
    but there's a war in the ice-box
        if you need a pick-me-up

        it's d.i.y.
        as sky falls off cusps of rust
      off such able arms of worm
    and into a sump
    round pegs in bauble sulk
done to touch paper sheen
    the lit earth still humming
    zephyrs blown to a floss

    the stars so starry
        howling arf arf bauhaus

    oh Thermidor

Aggropolis

Rampart of early kin
gdom, lamp hand can
no more surly, but as
worsted lands decry to
most governable parcel,
as to wold civil squall
aurochs abound in not
them as wont, carse noy.

Thane & carls & carline
willing able fief reivers,
rangers of their dogger
lone crust to derby stars,
so vassal span to glass
in minor modes, what
diffuse trickles burn own
grands off of apex argot.

Arrant? I nearly lost my
half heid shantil shining
though the lame is way,
which than mune is worth,
bang clannish as but kin
could no more grip fringe
than teeth rankles mak a
moment too too cramasay.

Coronach the mak undid
in cordial griddle burns,
a sack of sword firing to
a river's rough wooing,
so tending extremities
whereunto ye may reach
ample scarcement, fuse
crux to steelbow now.

This too, too barren pit
y gallows, rough shod
rise do plunge back all,
semper strong to bake
o local magnate, corbie
conner, flox, manrents,
a chisel home none durst
taste so striving sunders.

But from our throat band
each one to boaster skull,
a whole brood bought and
sold for some quiet death,
there native shafts to serf
through keen run pestilence,
a third off all churl, a dirt
canker of lank blown land.

Exceeding cruel, mingle
speir hemmed in to style
as a boot on other foot
loose felt a margret rose,
a taxi, mum, what wedge
there calling asserts its
ainmaist equilibrium as
a fringe now all to burn.

Back a hammer lens do
great jessie smithereens
to bolster bless arraign,
not prickle state of mars
in ready armour wards,
auld antonine crumbles
haps in rage to ditches
farflung een to danzig.

Renegades saw broke
men go, the going is
sure primogeniture to
a trace of shedding so
seldom sacked in old
sense or auld kail dosh,
said but spelt like read
lays never said fer awe.

Negleck nocht but to flee
curls oer seas, oer muling
chiel clock, the never ripe,
that seat of learning curve
to whey & splinter grey,
vehement against idols,
caw, caw mid a grave, a
set fair but for the grace.

Brethren mort dues cure
soul fonts, hook & crook,
a took fire noblesse oblige,
piety so mother smothered
in wanton cloth dochters
to seed a tipping bath but
whipped up rabble beefy
gin bondage of strangers.

Largely dead letters shine
heretic forth & kale stunt,
bell bent on fleeter dash,
as caress but tools o rift
to sun amok gaunt cries
as jasus and no quarter,
severed sore, a rip stone
to flounders blue in print.

Thorns out of pulpit be
the luggis lurid knuckle,
pillory and darling dross
under vane and fruitful
stool, fouls no flesh but
durst no pool of handfast
where but sent fine section
shocks fall, wave or crow.

Wish art burns a stake,
owl to dawning oar, so
little prophets its gale,
galley dusk welt scarry,
civil rapture & salve tar
to jeopard lives in ash,
heart singing apostatic,
a force of law, a mass.

Doth corn among chaff
rest except thou repent,
o monstiferous empire,
we espy not the flame,
decks above thy skin
coats death did so enter,
ensign chant of circe
in thy hot displeasure.

Linen & skins ring back
a swell pitch to mix some
shewe of civilitie, these
other alluterlie barbares,
no civil plant in roomes,
sic colonists then drive
a wedge between celts,
kintyre bludie to antrim.

Clamp fro plangent isle
to plantation of ulster,
laity tree carbon bound,
as thou o lord onely art
deservedly more master
than my sel, who would
had lesse been affected
in irelands & sad estate.

Gall vinegar of falsity
and contempt with the
cups of my affliction,
cyclopick monster as
fears utter extirpation,
tenants in battle array,
true banditti reappearing,
barrel o brandy on staff.

Beyond a head dyke, all
as round a rough bone,
rig torn so weedy baulk,
neer moves a mountain
diffuse in clachan haze,
seeks oatfowl eenbright,
pristine mid light wattle
going to but blank stane.

Struck dearth murrain so
to blooding the laird's ky,
visage scorn, as for want
some die, a wayside flux
shifts its flaming ague,
plague in a white cloud,
flea daunce o black rat
lays on of partly waste.

Glade poverty turns light,
stood on brink of great
jenny & water frame &
mule & throstle carding
engines gin scurvy blest,
potato mirth akindling,
a cruel havoc dauncing
thro kail & leaf & croup.

Marks of tide, a radical
wash hung liberty high,
dreg silver in our cups
as no sanguine rabble,
no sir, nor a down tool
to turkey-red dyes, tar
to coal, naphtha starch
wearing veins of jasper.

Canals into the drill of
the lag, rolls so rent to
cast transplants, stook
bitter on summit entails
their tapering heads do
cut and turn, flail sabre
in shag dragoons, your
virgin heart so burning.

What a way to cast clods
on kindred spirits, there
the sulk is on, you take it
all in, and chew mildew
like there's no wake left
and no worm, each head
of jawfall in calm lore as
so forth serries this waif.

But hither, crash viol,
the loose twang in gas
and halter, its sermon
ever falters, never no
fine tooth in sundries,
schmo labrets, there's
hurt to your elbow, so
gone on open mouths.

The taint of the carving
is in the slummy blood
of what grows feebler
in sulky grace, miasma
riding over, getting out
while the going is bad,
so less of that colossal
cheek & maiming sou.

Stark & stacked so bitter,
what crocks of shedding
on a tide of nails, pins,
even to base metals and
no end of toil, no don't
go on, leave off, hunger
to a rage, buried in bone
shackle to palpable scar.

Worse is come under in
inclement skies, before
each dark spit takes you
to water felt upon awes,
dusts down in pig iron,
swan of arc-light, flock
done to sparry feather,
ember gorse in dolefuls.

In wet soil, crisp white
scale holds to its mire,
what drip stalks, such
cut swathes, the rumble
slump and insert larks,
its best lie deep, steady,
the number dogs do lay
a dirt trail in each script.

Blue moon on fed day,
smiles so still, or soon
dies, drops a halo, hot
suits of nuclear electric
on th'ensanguined suns,
garb o grime, in rails of
bleached bondehede, no
ash of its worth or page.

O fucked city, its agon
lustre in foamy rind, to
do so soft with then on
acrylic afternoons, our
one good eye flowering
me with disaffections,
ah mine hurt, it shrinks
from less, it shrugs on.

As bake or dearth into
star cot, let's lie lower
love, let's lie low until
no dark so comfortless
blight of agent can still
wager head against our
rotting core, as they do
expatiate of this or fall.

Have you left my ear to
locks, a field of night in
the mine, ivresse as this
hair kindles into meteor
or blows of die, a mark
as fur or as sark blisters
rent asunder, its moral
streaks in fiery blesses.

So flower the baby for
pure boot and spur, to
list with zeal on banner
sky, each bright light is
you, for the taking, our
surfing oxide, treats of
burnished ore, its civil
song so shiney in wax.

You stand on a floor
of noise, its broken
vessels turning to a
savage lavender, the
soles flying through,
as so stuns a face to
unfold in each nerve,
each slice that carves.

In strokes or gritted
hate, its proud beats
to your darker pulp,
so steer a stern, clear
out this dormant sky,
now so cool or crost,
and cut a dash, esprit
doux, out of all cry.

Tadpole Men

Gold fish on hot beds
   so dog star rumblings
do out smooth volume
   on stones or on burns.

Now feel a cold fish
   beauty where sizzles
scar each star tissue
   of out and out skies.

Or give way, wet fish,
   for kink and clinker
to glisten while you
   earn and call it day.

As pop eyed lobe fish
   takes off with a will
so bursts its wet sac
   till quick fury gives.

And flying fish fins
   do flap so fear sent
as to skip oer mud
   is flip flop and joy.

Steer true, bony fish,
   a jaw held high for
a silk purse of egg
   so bleeds its pencil.

Or turn, hag fish, to
   look daggers on spine
in ice ink of nerves
   done to a crisp tee.

It's no use, bat fish,
   drag a sunless bulb
off each biting bell
   to dine on lost toe.

So slither, pearl fish,
   this host of hot boils
clanks on to a dusk
   now tuned to silvers.

Double Yellow

Not for you the evening
star, nor the barbed hair

of golden stone, now as
long sleeves of the state

hold us aloft this gutter
in scarlit ways, the grit

on each blackening oath
trailing to a burn of fire.

Tooled high, our pool of
worm blaze and simmer

goes through all its stark
waltz of jam today, buds

of crimson sucked amid
the ducked stool, a swift

stitch combing the tangle
to a long imperious quiff.

When did each curl talk,
the railing rises given up

to a scarfield, so blown
to orange jets and laced

cocktails, its comfort rag
spilling a tempered lawn

where the technicians of
sensibility plough on in.

Boulder of ruffled cheek
choke your callow sash,

with clutching temper in
legions the colour of our

ribbon or lung, systems
theory with a smile, this

stain of the local to some
drum and flower of ditto.

Night Night

A goose bump shrinks
from high, bare places
to a stung, prone oh so

supine hem, its lounge
short of fiery loam but
tuned to fine leaves of

ouch. We're rapt, even
as a sang rind and bark
enskies the miraculous.

So off with flits to an
inkling sulk, to glitter
for a pouring crag of

scoffed milk. Unsew
such spurious sorts to
ring in sweet chunder

or snores. If and only
if turns a lip canopy on
its fetchingly high side.

No, that brags it most
which throws to wake
off this filching. You

are some clear day, as
the yoke singes into its
neck. Spoons chrome

to chamber lines, white
trash all but blown into
love oer the core sloth.

Now rends out to deck
its joy boy, he of craven
dances, skirts and crust

cuts of mister bombast
scooping up scars in the
scouring. Be our sleep

collar, be our iron hum
to none, done for by the
moon in gorgeous bone.

Well, that makes some
crime of it, or simpers
into a windy but vogue

harangue, so sparkling
to the lees. Go swift to
dull, buds that oh stills

to trimmers or breaking
bounds, that optimum
slurp clasped in a pyre.

Tome

The cage rattles, it is
    some other, quick fire
in ills, filling out pain
    strokes through whirl

and seam. I would go
    in love's blows to your
hoping deeps, so deep
    you could lose an arm

in its bindings. O sad
    earth, it still gives, it
reaps that hair scarf
    and unwraps its lips.

So shine to the wall, a
    bole of bile and broken
charm, its clearest day
    filled with rue. Where

this humid spore gives
    in open pool, there the
delights eclipse, smoke
    in me doth reign, and

now draws fire. This
    carcass is of mine, turn
sunny side up, so flush
    to this plank of sun rot.

Less said, the worse, of
    which the meanest part
and worth folds its very
    smile. Hang an upshot,

switch on to all its light
    possibilities for notes in
rogue moods. What tan
    sets a face against each

bucket of scorn, a state
    of hiding teeth, now to
flip in rock and park, o
    gags and in committee.

Something does to a
    verdant lash of chill,
to decks of colour. It
    will not suffice. You

bathe with some night
    of plate, evening spills
spread out against an
    ironed dross. Then to

break from a snug fit,
    each radiant crust, in
good tenure too, now
    to vice come file away.

Shifts in wounds, proof
    and soggy hurt where
love blurts out a horrid
    truth. It can't be taken

in, nor will this tie into
    wealth tape. You do low
in yourself, so let down
    in more flocks of talking

points, that quick and
    poor tune. It's not for
me to say. Hark, the
    antique air is smiling.

As It Were

Mouth off to plunger, what farm
to little necessities glues these
   the fish to lovely, as whom food
unveils to aftermaths. On light
times untabled bulb arrays you
   come to feel its pinch, and are
of calls to sterner stuff, not one
but all told, leastwise that one
   off and folly sparkling wine bib.
But what more, what have you
to rainbow quips, slop shapes in
   late trash. No then, so thank me
furious one, done in great on fast
jibes, far from the wherewithout
   of folderol or gun romance. Make
ash bowls in this person as a cup,
teacake half best to last, no after
   you, but not to rarefy its passing
save as things fit. Do me out, my
love, in enough to be going on with.

One treats and coins with
the best among, how shine
is but that opened grotto

as what professes, as this
nude also takes the early
bath between the figure

of his donator and loose
of an as it were stammer
purple, lute of crater gum

Anyway but anyday
each and all on high
fans in no better scar

who could its novum
and normal temp on
singular ample, hip

to the nem con nods
of scary lux, cull me,
I am neither worthy

nor notwithstanding

And out of dominion
wake the silver string
to a lowly crime rate
and bagged flat, the

first come to, nor dare
to wield, shafts from
cloudy blandishment
to some honeyed bard

made on limpid ream
array, and is no more
master of the rolls nor
of these myriad locks

Yes, yes, I own as much,
   love the graceful swim
and would scatter lies
   to bring commissions in
how its tongue at least
   denies. S/he storms to
willing where a mimic
   ocean sets the terms for
lucid limbs. And who so
   bright as a transparent
gale turns the seminar to
   all soft confusion, weak
heads in pales of closer
   fold concealing, chatting
for all the dead long day.

In which passage
the thigh drops
from off bled

and if you do
but think it worth
can each fabulous

rise off of world
and fall confuted

Steady of feed bones
as it lewdly adds
or wings go weary

to a most ruly place
frank to last
stuck to the earth

as to its sticking place

Thence as to axial palms
shun the set out, a pencil
  dawn envelope, dog stall
and affiliates taken to a
steel more glitzy. Placid
is firm nearness, the licks
  of favour on of old to late
off waxen table books, the
very boudoir on slow ticks
and styles of bone in uses.

Off vocal grove, backwall
    leapt in steals of trip, trip,
then booted double turn of
    feet come to crash. How to
lend credence to the name
    in hand. Is there something
amid the numbers, a room
    to swing an amaretto, falls
as sweet as the hands fell
    so tuned to humming knees.

Then flits by dark kettle of
    beaten night, halls among
winces taking on themselves
    a fast toe. Sticking plasters
go under each duvet shivers,
    a freeze of primrose garden
to what long call are you
    so far from here, now it is,
seems so shorn of argument.

The pile driver rings
in late memo flasks,
ristretto fire, in goes
to Monday, when to

a weak shift there's
but a flower in your
open look, a feeble
task force through to

take of day, tasto solo,
this throng of down
sizes jogging holdalls
for a high water clerk

call it a day off

The larkspur gives to belly
   armour, a sheen repellent,
holding their job who reels,
more for out sourcing, o yes
   if music be, nor dance shine
sweet all, nor would go tear
to lingo, near to what will
   you do me on that, sip awry
I grant, but feel its heritage,
its cloth to warm boot loads.

Of dish, can no quicker plum
take you fancy tied, romper
   song on bangle dance, febrile
welt and went. One suppers
with empty thickets, pays
   what compliments of hosts
as go too far on kinds. Visits
wear to this, as if to some it
   is given to matter, and not
as an idle income, their rich
scream. O what au pair for
   short shrift can ask for ease
then leave amid their cups,
can as just lit, with no issue,
   take all it is, all but trusts
flung on urchin bacchanals.

For only in this can assess
disease, from its good core
skill and cheater soft lob
frame serum off a fashion

what like of thine but in
brilliant landlock berths
so falls silk of the crass
to a flip flower & carpet

where its trough is filmy
repeats nothing like the
haunting in blurry flairs
as thence partakes of us

And in the breeze of when a
    light and wonder, why does
this kindling dry, but of stale
    and there without a break
so that the reach is far over
    and this darkness forwards.

They hate of dull beetles, a
    stubborn wheel away, such
squills to calm and in few to
    reapers of the field perplex
or in the cooling wave, till
    the foot of the chair bleeds.

Envy unveils its late league
    tables, or brings you to your
senses, brings you to exercise
    a right to buy. The postal
district thrives into a very
    salivating figure, but alone
still in its malodorous barn.

Throw but the rub once more,
  now through the melts cotton
of such even decoration, now
  in pillow mantle, in trembles
for its autarky. Folds of the
  scene turn much put upon, blow
darker to fine off its belated
  double star. One might say
wrong as rain, delivered for
  who in vain claims sovereign
but never attained with, you
  can but eat shoulders & load.

Pleased with the found, so
        thrice earth defy'd, look to
sparklers in the brittle vent
        and yet one further thing
most pressing, come of this
        deadbody, as if some go
for we who are only, we
        who still but sums.

Epithalamion

amid the glamour of the secular and frankly godless hall
it falls to song to shimmy on down and sing it like it is
or would be if the law of speech acts did not beg the question
what ought or is can tether art to the greater promise of love
in short, where's Bacchus when you need him now that Pan
is just the god of silly sheep and savage earth can splash
the hour in flowers till the sheep come home without letting
slip more than a kiss of lasting bonhomie and not that
open song where love tramples on the slippery powers
of church, rite and the Lévi-Strauss memorial kinship shuffle

but come now, savage earth, dazzle the patriarchal sky
so open love can saunter through each warring thought
and furnish room where two can live as one, if not quite
united then dodecaphonic in their radical harmonies
you see, we're short of tone rows that don't sound anxious
now that rime's gone the way of the dog collar and there's
more than a splash of cringe in words like bride and groom
and that old plot which equates husbands with farmers

I think it was Hector Rottweiler who thought marriage
might be the last chance saloon in which to shape bonds
against the prevailing hymn-sheets of inhumanity
but there's a whiff of dogmatic hair-shirt under that collar
as if Proust had the last word on prisoners of desire
when you and I know that true love means never having
to say whose turn is it to do the washing up? or blow me
if freedom isn't the conscious recognition of necessity
which reminds me, now that Marx has replaced God
as the author of the Holy Family, it was Karl who
claimed that this relation lets us grasp how far
human nature has become, well, human nature, has
reached, that is, its most individual, most social being

this is hardly the song with which to practice duets
of private bliss, but if freedom as marriage can
only become general with the abolition of capitalism
it just goes to show that the dodecaphonic tone row
is no bed of roses, as we hope for roses over Mill Road

in the wish for more reciprocity than just giving gives
it's a comfort to be told that the planned economy
lives on now that Habitat has a centralised list:
may you be showered in soft furnishings when potlach
is but a wink in the eye of fiscal probity and may sun
clear a path through those clouds of ideology in which
RAE plus TQA equals SFA: no, we wish you better,
more human things than are dreamt of in that philosophy

call me a young Hegelian, but there's spirit in the
making when one plus one is more than two, a family
of more than bright ideas, as efforts to be in another
come to a chorus of recognitions too subtle for others
to more than wonder at, and it is wonderful, as we gaze
into the future, see you happy and hope it's a sign
that we'll be happy too, happier still if we can share
in your joys long after the moon's made of honey

familiars

i.

melancholy of a style grace
hence the room only when
s/he shines a whole cloud
copy as in no. 5 above, sad

and intricate, long to tone
that quiet will to squeaky
bubble wrap or neck shine
of span grey and meal into

circles of his pictured arm
knocking stance till when
it is stranger to tights and
sunk to all affronts so tall

ii.

because it is die a secret
die by she breaks her wings
stills to conversing on the
done thing, come as patient

with morning of glass sky
to accented beating or sails
that ever shed to the event
of dreamy parthenogenesis

and revolting union of this
tracing ways across defiant
stones, abiding in parallel
to bring the point home

iii.

to its application face in a
day's fruition and folly of
jacket on to a sprung floor
not in so many words but

s/he where it gives to open
rending the slick biddable
do as can but needs pluck
and you do as you do spark

terms in the domestic open
where the bright car studies
amid the day fall against the
bark blue of feeble kinds

iv.

sure blinkers of material in
bracketing out monumental
purrs appearing in the sight
and its passing of great mirth

as the plangency of its scalp
bids for inertia and affective
to the point of becoming dry
then lighting for this strange

bridge and making headway
are empty fires almost bright
but genetically fresh produce
for the jostling inch to inch

v.

to be camera high, as pencil
scores but a trace in the sun
for the found texture to crow
over and do away with crews

projecting the left over pastry
place whose laughing lines to
polished glasses the tinkling
of each smile gives new parts

at least if the moon of chrome
turns to hear a way through
the usual spokes, hand held
to blend in the merging scar

vi.

and the louse goes ouch to
the mother of all spiders in
from its grinding petal, so
shrewdly says the v-neck

attending to the nigh court
of the dim and loopy shake
that's noun high to stat
plumes in scart curvature

sliding down off the data
bone bind and sheer lucre
who spools their nerve tints
but stroked to fillips of pool

vii.

having a mazy run whose
membrane rag glues hooves
and all the nelsons for leaf
and lifter flowing wild with

just off hundred blue whose
cut penny gem always said
come charter its glad rink
under a guild of glove plate

through the humour and
the bulb of what's suddenly
the riding harm of darkest
saffron, noise aside a grave

viii.

shoddy in shambles bundled
through the corpus snags in
loose but sweet bother and
can you hold the good frond

that heads the field so spick
and preyed upon to fevers
of leafy coral, ice and legal
balustrades in scarf wounds

whose spearing but sunny
can steel all but the urgent
places of drafty and ample
that does for the ripped aim

ix.

well it beams lobe to fluff
bouquets and litter, swift
skinny ears shedding round
its sane yellow pales, thrown

light handling the white bar
through fiery bun of indoors
to span knots of parquet skirt
where did you pick that one

off to have the use and spur
her mirage, wrong foot off
tons of get you on, bubble
that glasses on to gone coo

x.

physique says it all thumbs
savouring the postage nose
as loveliest peelings flood
the fun diet of camper bags

whose brass licks walk spleen
to spokes of evening downpour
the fabulous orange off zoos
to sure blue iris, now steady

and suddenly the fixed shape
sheds its stoney carriage and
suffuses a fat of late that's
quite so on a butcher's block

xi.

another big hair do, quick
polls to the abominable so
enjoins s/he chimeras where
full on is no for starters

such smalls, a spruce herald
then shed destruction songs
crumb tenders for surely not
doing a stroppy rasp by the

scruff and glaze that dazzle
for which cf. the vignettes
regarding an unsightly wall
now dumb to any blind bruise

xii.

the lure so inflamed and had
flinched from speed to cheap
nor for the matching towels
as our splendour clinch left

for a soubriquet loosely done
come blows of dogma to bounce
stipples that spoon our veil
and that larded hint leaving

a veritable nest of machines
in some purple tinge as would
sweep hormones into the floor
were it but a brush with art

xiii.

now that's torn it, shredded
light as bowls of air space
cast that dusky scowl marked
for attention to the glaringly

obvious as to take that harsh
to task is that grown pathos
and his nibs set to pamper
even a withdrawal slip which

does our head in jumping for
the season of honey shades in
its new black, another shrug
and the floor's an old desert

xiv.

but what creases till tumult
fitting rooms to hot creeds
and pants of a grand mean or
her kind eye on a steep size

and number rounding, on hold
for the focal ache of wounds
not that candid prospect to
cymbals and Venus with arms

held for swan lifts above the
package plinth, no but wonder
which gets her bust then just
browsing in its eaten frieze

xv.

as while s/he gazed upward
the scruple of banter balks
its lines and veins as had
our scratch of passive good

taking a fume of subtle but
frankly wasted needle sport
that biff and boff won't do
for the coddling bruises in

also they prove our cyphers
of arrow if but hit upon by
nods as there are two things
in each revel of startling

xvi.

of which not the least sand '
comes some silvering of lids
shaved in wrinkles of a pull
sewn to sheds of bled balance

and daubed with bossed cuts
from sepulchral reels, where
so to lark in the short wing
call each toy our politics   .

of which not the shattering
but local colour, plumes in
moving pyres and the rest of
longing and a spilling clasp

xvii.

some question's posed, falls
upon the bowl of the city
like aspersions, each proof
shirty and calling the table

a branch of plastic vetted
after the bees circling the
wrinkling image in teams of
oblivion, my bubbly little

hormones of darkness, and a
palpable want of carnage to
hang out with the flora and
horizons set bang to rights

xviii.

darts slip to sour as each
beholder pounces on the hem
and trails, a swelling torch
to glaze over the meadows by

what's proud but gleaned as
if a dance upon the soiled
making struck to its proper
coil, the putting on of each

tooth to gritted light'ning
come clerical palm, splash
or what have you, bar none
if hardly worth the pouring

xix.

the thing is as the staples
hand and wrung from wrists
to fill the sky with capes
and washes, like tempers to

their warranties and brawls
come grieving then carpets
show weeds, its real estate
the savage lustre swapped

for bright beads and string
to drink in cheek, a stock
of our each and several but
close to blander eruptions

xx.

but as your splurge to flip
hardly does for a portable
smile cannot do but turn off
then how much for the love

of soot and scorching fills
the dirt has depth or still
beauty, well the spread took
off flush for all that daring

and a little of what does to
gloom on dolls anon or loopy
clips from point blank range
and a plunging rill of socks

xxi.

so what, the kidder's at it
for the praying screen comes
to as a dishy fulminator in
all or nearly all the burns

has to hand it to you, field
of ribbed footnotes and with
quirks ironed into the very
cool of the evening then lit

by the digital whack as that
blind in war's proud ensigns
and wrinkles of this lump or
a spark but nifty once over

Troubadour Unbound

Pound et toi, mon ami, mon
hypocrite professeur, camarade
de poésie, now here's a wonder
done out of the chilled section
best left to irrigate the parched
stones of the Orange Room, here's
to the return of the silver hounds
oh roll over there Swinburne
so indiscrete when numerous
when the bottle bank's hungry
and many a dog-eared index
card gathers rust in the greying
vaults of research fitness clubs
where the latter-day Thoreau
might take a leaf out of death
and profess himself more than
a little pleased by a hard day's
slog on the word-processor,
no, not now and not for us
there's more in them thar Cantos
than is dreamt of in TQA
and however you shuffle that
forcefield which repels as often
as it attracts, the thing is
you're a guide in the valley
of the one-eyed pro and just
so economical with the truth
that bruises can be as purple
and though poetry's a mug's
game with nothing in it, we're
in it together, come crime
and carping critics, however
the much vaunted nursery waltz
of usury and Medici gold
might be really spoiling us now

we'll leave the church-spotting
to the Renaissance blokes
and turn once more to song

The Prince of Bad Air

come zipper codes
      come date the shade
the mooning round wine-rucks
each sylph in sandals
as his silver streak machine
       sups on bloke soup
staggered through

to bullet points

pints   as solid phantasm
of corn   but ye dogs
   of cupidity   woof
am dozy libidinal
       let's slip
one over the bar sign

beaming from armpit to armpit
yawns to grace leisure
swinging bosom in negligee
distray   a cheese dreamer
    in his dogged   schmooze
vultures round her bloom
    whose fade to rotundity
leaves the woolf   to pale
   in the pink   going puce to floral

Amis comme cochons

knees brush as the crack is of
enlightenment and of some
interminable digression the like
of which betokens majesty

as when the theory boys
come marching in on ice
hipster that's slack dialectic
with a gift for high darkness

her amplitude as canvas for
our minor embrocation through
seams soft as clouds of putti
so rub the denim engines but

cannot bear too much hippy
ham fabric rips till on the t-shirt
AMOR VINCIT OMNIA calmly plunges
into your still attending jaws

Seasonal Greetings

another December morning does alarm time
stonily advancing towards boot camp hilarity
with the DJs, and what if several mornings
could stretch out south and fly the week
a flock of buses all at once taking the easy
way out along the trans-Europe express
while you, me and assorted vultures prey
on scripts like the falling of the weekend
into someone else's arms, someone else's
pocket. Xmas is coming, relenting cheers,
Xmas is coming, well did it ever leave the
cupboard stuffed for the eternal return and
no we don't recall the siege of Leningrad
save in the most pressing of food queues
while the DJ cranks up the contempt bass.
There's no ice on the inside, which is good
only a tickle from central heating to meet
the chorus of mobiles and sheets smiling
somewhere there's a contract out on you

Cut to the Quick

who as it were in the very pink
can saunter above petty cash
in yet another faultless expo

come spills to greet the guests
so warmly, with such obliquity
that will do for me till day's end

and later, fresh from the news
of a quite previous masquerade
the crooked elbow has its say

taken to number off like some
sweetner held to corrupt the
sweetest teeth among staples

but off! off! ye floral chemises
let fly in your pacific loafers
such stark and soapless arias

that get up on the brush off
out of shapely dancing as we
who are about to lie salute you

100 Days of Mammon

he walks, he talks, and then
some, and there is murder
in his eyes where once a wind-
capped orator flew off a shiny

plate of still to be assembled
loves and sang of old the killer
sound-bite so chuffed on song
going boom boom so few uhms

per drift it's the way you tell
them disappointments to keep
like how you fell in with lamé
slipper crews en route to slicks

or gems re the half-wept stare
that's so broke why fix me up
et le rat a mangé le biftèque
who holds the fort as a beau

cirque du monde and nature's
a destructive principal that's
a fact cue extensive laughter
leaving beasts for badinage

and the zoo's so you it drains
slackers of public calamity
now some Chambre de Justice
holding out for singular revels

each to fuck an epistemological
squirm for a game of soldiers
done real low maintenance
that the nature of the gauze

is its purpose here today and
gone to Jerusalem flag happy
well in that sense I grant you
a kind of slide-show of Being

with woof woof in the lock-up
or bad flava so idolators are
topsy huh? weapon of choice
done calm and final warming

up to the task and even if I
too have insisted that there's
an idiocy to evil it's a spirit
of malice to make such specs

oh pants they boom to curl
up for spanking fine maths
and long primitive additions
hear how with cross'd thumbs

they play ave mum whose box
is flicker still for a back drop
ah me how does our grog go
will bloomer into such folds

to avoid the barking prizes
and a hint of spring wafters
a right shed-load of morals
what less could you wonder

nor I, not even attachments
yet more 3-d images, yawn
so still the water gently seeps
as if www.Noah.com's come

among us bearing glitterati
ooooh, the flatter the better
says yonder Monsieur Luddite
it is the thought that counts

indeed much appreciated
and the same to you, though
I say go! go! go! Mister 2000
and your many damp patches

come waltz said liberal circles
we're off to Barcelona to catch
a hint of '36 that still lingers
in the air amid the stench of

urban regeneration a.k.a.
kapitalismus the euro-way
then mice are lightly bored
but perhaps there'll be room

for another moody lunch when
the new year is not so new
though even in Derry there's a
franchise opportunity culled

from exalted necklaces of cloud
gone fable and fable that no's
not among the massing ranks
nor can be headed, never fear

all in for bonbon delicatessen
naked agronomists in Russian
for business so hot to forever
defuse the situationist in you

c/o the mother of all song with
this ghostly incisor in its flesh
syllable now you see it plain
to bury alive the flaming neon

bombarded to a picture skip
as if stars are acrid fools set
in whose wonder buck naked
sky this but turns to carry in

say-so or falls in with a moving
regime when you do 'human'
they take you for a humanist
of the sheepskin persuasion

larks from the razzle up low
who can't see for speakable
joys so strange in darks to say
nothing of your blistered looks

Ostrich Takes Off

flocked machines curl up on roughage
and run up tacitly the extreme savvy

felt to rumble and as the earth burns
what just in does off on cattle & horse

now ostrich flesh has the driving seat
right in there on joined-up burgerism

what convertible bond do savour each
I mean puh-leese if the *vice Américain*

is so becoming then the *Sprecher* can
take the first hike among said equals

let the mission steaks go fuckabout
or more sooth on horde or lard lounge

run to blunt risk glades as you were
and wouldn't it be nice to stay clear

if not tight to the pterodactyl wind
plucky in pink among roasting birds

now summer's here and up in flames

Homage to Mayakovsky

Philologists,
        cyber-snouters, ye olde
                shit-stirrers!
from ordure and the tacky night
        deadlines are come again
                like agit-pop
that may tip
        your tongue to
                one more 'heugh, spit.
What more
        will our cognitive codgers find
                for papers
      to tut the curious
                thaws,
that are — well,
        hard boiling, tinctures of pulp
          those fluffy pups
             or friends who paste the heat.
Right then,
        off with your fancy optic, prof bloke,
        take a turn on categorical
                    intuitions
        and why not, so unlikely —
moi,
    foot and mouth butcher
            now pump primer
finds the call-up,
        nay sanctioned for lost elections,
                freezing on the edge
of drooling pastures
        where the silver spoon mobs
             are hot for more silver.
Not so, Aurora
    (her, the no-logo whore),
            old cradle snatcher
   of many a maiden pamphlet

and worse
umbrage,
              fivers,
                        datcyls for line dancers
morning puke and the dawn choir
                              quelle horreur!
Our savage bird-fancier
              does his cheeky cataloguing —
he'll check out each sweet digit
                    tout suite,
                              you mark my scars
now feathering the flames
                  lest the anthological beasts
                              refine harm
          into fist-flights of a sorrier syntax.
But what's to do?
              amid power plants humming
                    the seven veils of democracy,
      what savour to pare?
                              or cull to carp among
our software
                  vacuum packed herbs
                        city heights and private skies
                              the social on sale
          like lost leaders and a co-op funeral.
Moi aussi —
                running the messages
                              leaves chowder
      where the critique of slick taste
                        browns and foxes at the edges.
Lighten up!
                comrades of the posthumous,
                        here's another quiver
                              felt-tipped quipster
                  showering the poetaster anon.
We'll crash the lank
                  and second-hand songsters
                              as quick for it
      as any lunging theorist —

[98]

we'll come unto you
            unAmerican activities
not like the mission statements
            or retro Celanians
who know the local, but too well!
            our whispers will tickle you
                        over pain and schism,
      over quiffs of choirs
                        and committees.
The ruins will mumble on
            with a not-so-Tintern sparkle
   (con gaz)
            but with the lippy
                        in Cupid's lyric dash,
not like the footnotes
            under the curator's fondle,
      nor with the reviewer's
                        belated charms.
These damaged goods
            will find their way
                        among remaindered pyres
      and lucid,
            risible,
                        irrepressible,
                        share a pillow with you
as are with us still
      the public spas
            etched in lime facades
                        so shaded with acid.
These snatched
      of fossil songs
                  join the lost pines
and are cut out for
            pronounced ire
                        contra 'National Trust',
so livid with alienated labour
                        and slips of death dues
      that each flat moth
            lost to itself in electricity

will flame
        and then combust
                in the halo of obscenity.
Et voila —
       in party togs our nouns undress
   and skip through
           the prosodic scandals
                on tender toes.
There shift the nibbles,
               grim with e-numbers
     for sacrificial finishes,
         thermal loads ascending —
              and to attention.
Pint-glass to pint-glass
            heaving over belted horizons
the heavy dudes
       arrange
          their deadly extended sequences
  with an epigraph too far
            seeping from each side-pocket
and the much-loved
         arsenal of lathed put-downs
             saved for the bar exercise
         of critical snap
   chop to the knees on the qui vivre
           to explore the wounds
  with puns and quips
         and all the fire that envy breathes.
And all this army
         armed to the false teeth
     with years of weasel blinks
           to their eternal credit
and then assembled
        for some thumping majority:
     we throw it around, then away
           the civic globe and co.
Tribune
      of the slumbering proletariat
               (who s/he?)

that's ours all over
        scorned,
           mourned,
               bosomy too.
All are called
      under the troubled
          down years of realisation,
we've done the Gesammelte Schriften,
            like you do,
  as an analysis of fridge remains
        to dance over each best-before,
and even without shelves
        we could aver
      with whom to muster,
         a side to call our own.
But negativity
      came of its own
         not out of Adorno's hat.
Over dinner and afters
        what whistles among our robes
when memos set managers to howl
    the very howl
      come harlot's cry
        that ran down office walls.
Let that bitch Cereberus
      show his teeth
         to Hektor Rottweiler
so stirs the
     same again,
        and one for yourself?
Die,
   die, my text,
      like any temp or co-worker
left for dead
     amid the station-wagons
        of the photocopier.
Sweet nothing
    we give
    to boast 'exegi monumentum' — pah!

sweet nothing
                for pebble-dash cladding
                        for gold leaf on the spine!
We're in this species together
                        let's get it on
        out of shambles
                into the liberties
                        and lay down the ruins
        of social being
                a.k.a. the long hike to socialism.
Philologists,
                fasten your lexical life-belts,
        we're headed for a bumpy ride
                down the glassy surge,
                        when recherché items
such as 'arbitrage'
                'drug tsar'
                        or 'serotonin'
        swim as filaments of tumbleweed
        hushed into the nuclear winter
                        of our fathers —
                how green do the valleys become!
For you
        of iron lung and buns of brass
        who's left?
                but those licking their wounds
                        those taking turns
                on this treadmill
                        or the kit that walks.
So through a train of tears,
                we're half way to popsicles
                ice-men
                our fossil songs
                        left for slurry and screed.
Come,
        universal songsters,
                let's step up on the quick foot
                down the long stairwell
                        to the end of days.

There's hardly a note
                    left in the drawer
                                barely a floppy
        or rich-text format
                        sculpted for perishing
and, to be frank,
                mes amis
                        the undercarriage may fail.
That said, I'll swap you glory
                        for the sustain pedal
called on
        by the Friends of St. Just
                    our crimson-headed dancer,
out beyond the thumping throng
                and those fellow-travellers
                            of Trot and Gentry,
but we'll stay up eh?
                    like flexible friends turning
leaves of conversation
            from each to each
                    going one better than the night.

Smooch-Punk Fusion

sunk riff contra payola
it's a family affair now
Exmouth market calls
at the top of our dials

or going on something
over daring funk drole
fringes so stirring still
amid the balding lyres

take that you freebird
that dash of daft quiff
left to mingle with the
newest pringle jerseys

spangled chevron turn
to rusty jacket braces
set to the continental
dorf disco bus or angst

trims the strummer's
paw flaying those air
chords on dog drums
for the plastic chicken

so how you fought the
law and won a cheese
grin that tunes smile
riots in the key of life

[sic]

metallic tongue shivering
on for the wreathing year
so tall flops off how yes
turns night gales to nose
on costly string and lyre
for exultant mistress bee
who readies the scorpions
and so say 'raw' material

on the line 'good' nature
your pretty eyes away far
it's lonely knee up ahead
when to gentleman styling
who gives a shimmy and on
come strip the xmas scree
eg. kerms, chochineal and
dye derived from pickling

the irk of whose roots go
yield to great permanence
and the flame colour took
up easy peskiness for fun
run sicamour in cypresses
imperishable as flummox'd
that's putting it sweetly
to open the surgical acid

would o would on a hiding
quite meaning well but so
eccentric he could be our
virgin of department song
I just said her thing for
authorities sang piss off
to viols the calling sark
just into shorts that eel

of autumn on the raw neck
with purls or finger loop
in lieu of fallibilist to
reserve loss frenzy shock
fitted up right and girly
so that 'proper' does for
short work of an absolute
the schematism to fade in

we loved all things about
her especially the finale
tamping down off droplets
in zone to urban savannah
that hung corse whose eye
renews the wintering scar
it would but bruises glow
to run and mock the gloom

and the flying fuck's now
seen to lips and learning
carbolic in the start huh
setting all at naught new
my shoe rose and sore pip
for the tawdry takings or
what lasting sterility to
set jelly edicts to dishy

rack skint in shit furor
running for a priori top
stunning lack of politic
in the singular want gut
shell shacks in it minor
gruntest thou shimmering
for the bald ceiling and
evening's sewer bleeding

return to previous cream
in the fold closer scale
to skeleton army in this
night exotic half the ah
showing the during skein
timbre is as ramp breeze
lit to beat the pulp dog
calling on patriarch wit

and at the border mouths
each drawn vulcan patter
into the duck duck cower
fickle sauce held out to
faith for all the yellow
who shoulder the bathing
and each slight held for
the beauty as in leather

that's send for a blague
to fill in for furnishes
where escarpments cut in
deepest darkest lie here
by my side of cramp calm
and then take up to lift
fanning out fang goodies
drawn for one night only

rack visible then friend
and rails used for blunt
unto edge viz. man [sic]
is free and his will can
take the claim for class
into its fantasy leagues
to bland radical evil as
mysteries take for crops

by attempts then augment
happiness whilst barking
up their opposing torque
half and hard perfecting
who show the way to ripe
as in the romantic bodes
to be done well to other
and rare to mean radical

all our judgments blousy
bled to standing collars
the scarf worn to lights
and the potential wedded
to gadding about town or
stir but patience huddle
make your own colloquial
will can to flaming arse

the log does fitter duty
on to brunch parting eg.
more on the hoof for the
bog standard demos sinks
who rooms to the sploosh
with his paw munificence
in hurt suppers then put
down for mires on stucco

hand in hand the shocker
and cheating stock pales
before the up and coming
years he blew in promise
and another scare tactic
the film noir pragmatism
withering on pain coming
up like its notable curl

sweeping new measures

1.

hot foot to it finest of fine bit dead,
as they thought, the rash crinkle fires
when lax on scars they open in paraffin

and heads fell, shame each lost penalty
who takes up to run such as idiot booze
prevails the want or pupil lux too true

will you no take the bitters sonny dog?
and shoulder the vanity, shoulder frown
for each wee bit fire, dead for gristle

2.

till rid of light, the mountain rebound
grows treachery, nothing too grand mind
you and your mockery of the kitchenette

save succour and twine all flouncing on
stocking cloth taking its exception and
dim the dimmer, our very own ooh or aah

no pick one of the fit cloth finishings
spent on threads, bedside lexicons or a
fading fancy for the darker gong on oil

3.

is there no ripeness to her put me down
would tuck the slanging deuce upon each
little advantage in the flattery raffle

well all sorts, yes taken, or kept back
spank to loafer now bounces dawn to fly
show me that rise and I'll squander all

now hail the savage sparrows holding up
Venus to general motors as Vulcan ticks
set to worry the sheep grazing in maths

4.

while the truth-seeking pump going like
a clap slips down upon its knees to beg
to differ for 'modern' read 'human' for

swarming blazers yonder door for 'logo'
read 'logos' something for it sprinkler
and spring oral chorus grand for 'test'

read 'text' that's right vital burdened
with a wondrous palm upon the morrow to
flip on the least cry's fumbling morass

5.

hand, hard, not to mention vile in show
that goose du jour squeaking go on like
crème wasn't built in a toast, falls in

and her zip code said Beirut first drop
then check lark with the stripe pyjamas
spent en route to the Peshawar corridor

as spectacles of the best the aid could
subvent, may I proffer you another lick
as that done wing scumbled c/o Philomel

6.

therefore, how drole, what's so precise
more even than a 'surgical' strike thus
the bladdered dead sea for weekend blah

like you knew the personal plunder trip
was just a sap way of currying desserts
ferrying up tough-luck supper scenarios

one after another how we laughed, smelt
the coffee and dreamt in body liners of
sandbags at dawn, tides turning to beer

7.

then the caprice takes an unlovely side
for a bell-wether postulate, dead right
being without data along a heart string

vibrant, perm said to blow away the web
in its live-in plug, day's spent wonder
blended to hours upon relay, more crash

and darkest crumble our social services
in blood clots, plans to frisk even the
ballet fan rattling a cage marked Weber

8.

gripped by the mood and light pollution
by listing then a little bit barking or
shift dresses fitted and flaring all as

the demure set to expose more loopholes
in the palest latin of tracer fire then
ardent dusk slips hints at a late final

sweet nothing cradled for the love shot
go easy as fear encrusts the longer sky
and merest thunder comes as a trembling

9.

up to the integer bold of works dancing
to have some equivalence in Aristotle's
catalogue on the boo which was intended

what stop, use or efficient cause to do
some grist of the classic goal-posts on
the move playing location upon location

and men do alter as the birdland spills
from the UK negative territory to speak
then delete 'of them' before passing on

10.

mutter mutter re economic impact downer
did I hear mispoke by your minus growth
called like we see it to a frail breeze

at the same blind there's that stimulus
related to, and an aid to, stunners all
contra strident's strict flutter (yawn)

still, the mood has changed, portfolios
fissure into belly up tickled to a pink
and bacon rind, where the sheen is prim

11.

on the counter-cyclical play so to puff
clean up, showers of vibe as by crucial
you mean they are consuming confidences

set to serve the transcendental withers
blown around as hair days take the turn
for the ethos that most pampers the low

just a lard sump longing for a blessing
not that you take the fly blown platter
a.k.a. a new week off from t.v. dinners

12.

but that could prove a false smile, all
this as winter approaches, what refugee
can bare the scoundrel and shabby queue

hail to thee, ye bang to rights blinded
for a world food pivot making us a rift
as the topos shows up to remainder moi?

of course this does not save the bruise
while the phrase 'classical' passengers
takes a sharp intake of blonde romances

13.

and skinny fries with everything, totty
that holds sway before the unhistorical
do much as the tightly knit express ire

then principle surely triples antiquity
application pending, meanwhile upon the
village classroom silence falls for the

communiqué rumoured as intense pressure
would deflate all the learning left for
what they call a closed military buffer

14.

what fag packs in the bland and bulging
which are, limply, machines for a choir
whose yardstick is flung as a bee-sting

floating upon cycles of violence dulled
according to a cloud that does but seem
too lively when it's a gag on the cards

and when is it not, spilt brine barking
in the shudder, stank, sole to shingles
is that a place so simply left for home

Printed in the United Kingdom
by Lightning Source UK Ltd.
109998UKS00001B/104